I0796946

There are books that stain you long after you put them down. *In the Good Years* is one of these books; it haunts you, in the best ways, with its flea-ridden dogs, summers steeped in the self-knowledge of girlhood and honeybees and vexed familial lineages, the profound and profoundly painful moments of lives lived, shared, and shed. It's not hyperbolic (I hope) to say that the whole world is here—but unlike the actual world, Cresté's is cradled in pristine care, attention, and with language so deft and exact, it could have only been made. —Ocean Vuong, author of *On Earth We're Briefly Gorgeous*

In the Good Years offers a stunning archaeological dig of language, time, and intimacy. Cresté's poems excavate tenderness and violence, the personal and the political, ecosystems and their destroyers, treasure and trash, history and the multiverse of futures contained therein. Each poem is a site of meticulous, gentle sifting, each line a careful curation of artifacts. Cresté's radical attention unearths and re-earths, restoring context to its discoveries and finding homes for the unhomed. Breathtaking. —Tess Gunty, author of *The Rabbit Hutch*

In *In the Good Years*, Laura Cresté forges a speaker attuned to historical and familial forces—a speaker ravenous for communion, a speaker who notices the distance between people, the gaps in history. Moving from childhood to adulthood, these poems radiate with a translucent interiority. I could feel the speaker's emotional and intellectual growth, setbacks. Each experience, each glimpse of the world is rendered in precise and resonant language. In the poems that hold the dead and disappeared in Argentina, Cresté deftly braids familial narratives, political violence, translation, guilt, and survival into a tour de force that jolts the senses. Laura Cresté is a remarkable poet. I'm thankful for her first book. —Eduardo C. Corral, author of *Guillotine*

"Airplanes from opposite windows in their twin beds." "Bright smear across spoiled film," with "no / choice left but to let the lit world in." "The sea out of the sea." Debts. Dan's drunk driving. Egg sandwiches, "fur stuck to my tongue," a good boyfriend who enjoys "that poem / you wrote about your ex." An entire alphabet of the apparently ordinary made into lines that stand out like split geodes, from girlhood to quarter- or third-of-life crises, from "jelly shoes and jelly sandwiches" all the way up—or down—to wars and whales, "water welling gutters," and years lost to health rollercoasters and generic Zoloft—here is a whole life that some of us recognize, portrayed in sonic palettes that never tire and rarely even repeat, and sparkle, and shine. If Laura Kasischke has an heir, she's here, making do, throwing dodgy parties, converting demons into tentative friends with melodic hexameters or deviled eggs. Here, too, are the family legacy of Argentine rulers' cruelty, the ordinary harm of patriarchy, lemons and oranges, love of one kind and love of another, and memory, memory, Argentina, New Jersey, basement floods, supermoons. Here we are, and by we I mean the poet and me and you, any of you. Join us there. —Stephanie Burt, author of *We Are Mermaids*

In the Good Years

In the Good Years

Laura Cresté

Four Way Books
Tribeca

Library of Congress Cataloging-in-Publication Data

Names: Cresté, Laura, author.
Title: In the good years / Laura Cresté.
Description: Tribeca : Four Way Books, 2025.
Identifiers: LCCN 2025003846 (print) | LCCN 2025003847 (ebook) | ISBN 9781961897564 (trade paperback) | ISBN 9781961897571 (ebook)
Subjects: LCGFT: Poetry.
Classification: LCC PS3603.R48 I5 2025 (print) | LCC PS3603.R48 (ebook) | DDC 811/.6--dc23/eng/20250210
LC record available at https://lccn.loc.gov/2025003846
LC ebook record available at https://lccn.loc.gov/2025003847

This book is manufactured in the United States of America and printed on acid-free paper.

Four Way Books is a not-for-profit literary press. We are grateful for the assistance we receive from individual donors, public arts agencies, and private foundations including the New York State Council on the Arts, a state agency.

We are a proud member of the Community of Literary Magazines and Presses.

Cover art: Sean Landers, "Sperm Whale Skeleton" © Sean Landers, courtesy of the artist and Petzel Gallery, New York. Photo: Christopher Burke Studio

Book design: Maisonneke

Contents

Dead Horses

I like to imagine when horses were unremarkable
as Toyotas. When you wouldn't turn to your companion
after spotting them in a field and say "horses."

I'm alive because an ancestress on horseback
caught a man's eye on Ocean Parkway.
He followed her in his car; they married.

Across the hemisphere, my great-grandfather
hoisted his thirteen-year-old bride
onto a horse and stole her away.

When she saw her mother again, they were both old women.
But I wouldn't wish it undone.
I want to get born.

I never asked my grandmother what she loved
about horses—shattering speed, how their eyelashes
look human, that they're loyal as dogs but dignified?

She owned something like one-sixtieth
of a racehorse; she's not alive but Just Zip It still is.
I tell a friend I'm thinking a lot about dead horses

and she believes I mean dying, the broken
back in *Anna Karenina* or the glue factory.
No. I am thinking of my own dead and how

they were carried. Once saddled across a mare
named Ramona, I was afraid of the burden of my body,
that she would buckle—an animal once ridden into war.

I was a teenager and jealous of the freedom
I imagined belonged to the thin.
Now I know no one feels free,

not even the creature who devoured
the countryside, ravenous for the time
we were allowed in the field.

Overripe

Sometimes it's like this: slugs
discover the basil no matter where it's planted.
Batshit on the welcome mat. I cave in

the burrow between cherry tomatoes
and rosemary. Every day the chipmunks
dig anew until I fill the hole with sticks,

menacing as the Blair Witch.
After storms, I skim the drowned and stunned
from the pool. Today's accounting:

one dead frog; newts: three dead, two living,
flung far from where the late tomatoes split
lewd as Jesus with his bloody heart.

Mike tends to never-ending tasks,
neatening the yard of fallen twigs,
while I believe in entropy and let it alone.

We drive to the farm with corn stacked on ice.
At the ignition turn, a chipmunk crawls
from the hood, and we confound each other

through the glass. A baby. Glimpsed
and then gone. I wish I remembered the look of it
as well as I do the frog—its terrible skin,

clear coating sliding off like jelly.
Bubble taut across its mouth.
When insurance stops covering my birth

control, I give it up and feel slightly more animal,
sore breasts, and more so when I trade plastic
for a shampoo bar and turn greasy from the coconut.

The radishes never take. Snakes undulate
in the pool and leave their skins behind
on the stone wall, flimsy dresses I'd shuck off

as I climbed drunk into bed for years.
The therapist in my phone asks
if the meditation he prescribed is helping.

Does it matter? I just need
the summer to end, for the garden
to die back a little.

The Mothers

My aunt's husband left her for a pilot and my parents' marriage stalled when I was too young to notice. Eventually they'd reconcile, but for a while it was two sisters and their daughters; one worked and one watched the children. Our mothers were fourth and fifth children of seven. One brown-haired and one blonde. Thin as models because their mother smoked and would make a single box of spaghetti for dinner. One dropped out of college to live on a boat; teach English in Colombia; scuba dive at night, the jellyfish like lanterns. One married the boy she'd loved since fourteen. Each went to grad school twice. They say unforgivable things, then forgive each other. They teach us our phone number by singing a song. They teach us Miss Mary Mack; disaster preparedness; if you think he's cheating, he's definitely cheating, and if you *don't* think it, he might still be. They teach us never let him see you cry. Between them: three husbands; three daughters with soft, vowelly names; two sons an afterthought. The boys don't know our mothers the way we do—we met them when they were young and unmapped. When I snatched my cousin's drawing, a paper garden tearing between us, my aunt ripped mine in half, to teach fairness. The mothers fought wildly then, when we were simple enough to be adored. Before we grew up and became less comprehensible—not proud enough with men, weak, crying when angry. My aunt would say about her ex *I never once begged him,* even though they had an infant: a story meant to be instructive. About this they would always agree, though there were some months the moms didn't speak. They criticized each other's parenting. One loathed the other's husband. In their late middle age, I think of them as flowers once bent toward different suns. They speak almost in code, omit all proper nouns. They make me wish I had a sister, and I do have a sister. When they were girls, they counted airplanes from opposite windows in their twin beds. *I see one. I see another.* But it was the same plane.

Radius

What I know about bones is elementary.
        I know my grandparents' bones are decades

in the earth and must be revealed by now:
        skeletons in Sunday dress, hand bones emerging

from suit coat like spokes of a broken umbrella.
        In time, the interior of body meets the interior of earth.

The César Vallejo book my father pressed
        to his father's chest has settled into a ribcage dark.

The bony sounds—tooth box clatter, knee crack,
        neck twist—remind me where I've taken my body.

My wrist-snap against floor and a worse pain:
        the bonesetter's sudden pull and the long heal.

Bones are a wordless record—the break and the knit-back
        fracture a forensics team would know me by.

I took my bones to Paris and stooped through
        the catacombs. I touched neither the ossuary's wall

of femur nor lumpen tunnel of skull. It's obvious
    but worth saying: those bones were once beloved.

Bones built of mother, marrow, star, and milk.
    It's a privilege to know where your dead are buried

when it might have been otherwise. The mass graves in Argentina
    my family were not lowered into, they who made the unlikely

escape. My grandfather's name on the dictator's list,
    marked for death, yet who fled and lived, and lived, and died

in an American suburb, held by some of his children.
    I once held a choking child, not mine, upside

down and thumped the small back with the heel of my hand
    until he cried, alive. His ribs had the give

of a young wood, a tree that could grow beyond injury,
    swallow fences. I had never been so scared, but that was last

year and the child is still breathing. I've held my breath
    passing cemeteries, but now visit the village of dead

with intention, touch names with wings or a skull
 and cross, letters furred with moss. I know these bones,

live and flush beneath my skin, aren't white, but murky
 and many-hued. In the graveyard, the murderous

last century unfolds against marble or granite, dates aligning
 with war or with plague. You can read luck or money

into a long breath between years. Here lies one granted old age.
 Sometimes there's a family plot. Sometimes the story coheres.

Self-Portraits

Laura Ingalls, my namesake,
whenever industrious and doughy,
cutting biscuit rounds with a water glass.

*

Swallowing my SSRI,
the modern kind
of mentally ill, untethered
to hospital or bed.

*

Summers naked, suntanned, nearly
drowned. School years suburban,
the wake of a commuter bus rushing
against the walls of our house.

*

In the wasted years,
a secretary, stealing time
from the company and the good pens.
The graying square of a tote bag

daily kissing the subway floor.

*

A barber, the months in the country
hiding from contagion,
shaving my love's neck.
The crooked horizon of hairline
that confronted me each time he turned away.

*

Asleep under eiderdown,
blank and American.

*

Sometimes allowing sex I didn't want,
I was historical.

*

Drinking coffee,
for minutes at a time,

immortal.

*

Vacant reflection
in the pupil of a whale,
gaze unreturned as the back of a spoon,
eye no longer an eye.

*

Bright smear across spoiled film:
when a broken aperture cannot
withstand the sun, when there's no
choice left but to let the lit world in.

Inheritance

At the kitchen table, I sense woodchucks
beneath the floor, borders of burrow
and home slackening with dumb fumbling

sounds, till I stomp on their roof.
Months into quarantine, I call my father
for his roast chicken recipe. It changes

every time and is always perfect.
Two chickens ago he used half
a Valencia orange instead of lemon.

Now he and my mother aren't speaking,
but I pretend not to know. Instead, compare
animals: the black bear who circled the house

like an omen, my father's starlings
with their oily bibs. He offers stale bread,
then worries it's not good for them.

Mike and I walk every day, baby-talk
the goats penned in by the side of the road
in their oatmeal sweaters.

Until the day the pasture is emptied
of goats—wire fencing gone, grass bitten
to the quick. We don't know

the farmers well enough to ask.
We smile tightly and nod in the way
of New England; collect advice when offered,

such as: if you hear a woman
screaming in the night, don't
enter the dark yard. It's only the fishers.

We turn our ears to the night
with a clinical interest until we forget.
When the shriek finally arrives,

it comes from me. A clattering
thump, then another, and then I am
howling before I come awake.

You're okay, Mike shouts to be heard,
it was just a picture, a picture fell.
I don't know how to explain

the terror ready to rise up
from the expansive safety of my life,
as unsettling tea with a spoon

stirs the dregs to the surface.
It can't be because soldiers once
dragged my family from their beds.

It can't be, because my father
had already fled. Fear didn't
transmit through the genes.

I try to keep us safe in paltry ways.
Truss the chicken, sharpen the knives,
sharpen my ears for footfall on the stairs,

but it's only the woodchucks annexing
the underdeck. Weeks pass like this,
waiting for something we can't name.

For a long, stark time, spring feels near,
branch buds erupting, the nervous
scent of arrival. We turn over

the garden, decide we can live
with fear and do. Some days
I can make a perfect thing.

Slip the onion from its paper
clothes, salt the bird, yank
the thyme free, no need

to measure—it's nothing new.
People have been doing
exactly this forever.

We Love Bad Dogs

the way we love bad men.
No woman in my family would
admit this, but it must be true or else why
would we keep bringing them home.

We love dogs who draw blood
without warning, men who kick in doors
and call us crazy. It's not fantasy

about the power to change, that you can
love someone into kindness.
It's a simple gospel of staying, gold
estate sale jewelry and trading in your name.

We love like a sentence
that once given
cannot be rescinded.

In the blue glow of a crime show,
my aunt says If that were my father
I would still love him
and visit him in prison.

A *serial* killer? I prod, trying to distinguish
between crimes of bad impulse
and a real true joy in violence—ropes, knives.

Even then, she says.
Her tall, senile dog has scarred
two faces: nipped a woman's
chin, and worse, snarled open

the delicate skin of her nephew's brow,
requiring stitches, nearly
skewering the eye.

When explaining to my fiancé
how I was raised, I insist
on my own good sense,
claim to be different:

will not love what I cannot trust.
Yet when that dog, so tall
we called him The Horse,

approached me at eye level,
I did not turn from his clouded gaze

or black healthy gums
as he put his mouth to my cheek.

I'm not immune from wanting the rank
breath of the wild. I extend my face
soft with hope. I expect to be spared.

Sisters

Back when we were witches, and we said about the little one
We'll test her powers soon,
I was always having the dream where I climb
up a hill and then fall off the earth.

I'm grown now so I dream about the work waiting on my desk
and, under the desk, the mice.

I remember jelly shoes and jelly sandwiches,
Skin-So-Soft and No-More-Tears, our mother
burying arrowheads for us to find in the backyard.
When the shark head washed up, I held my breath
and tugged loose some teeth—

I'm always taking the sea out of the sea.

It was the summer my sister let the tomcat in, chipmunk
thrashing in his mouth, and our mother shouted
Jesus Fucking Christ so the neighbors never said hello again,

and the summer and the years of unsleep
after I found our grandfather dead in the cellar,
on the floor that was good for his back.

In time we forgot his voice and would swear
on his grave to make each other shiver.

We knew yellow honeysuckle was sweeter than white.
I kissed my sisters during *house*, and other games like *shipwreck*
and *mental institution*. Without a brother it didn't feel dirty.

In the outdoor shower, we'd press wet outlines to the wood
to see who was tall and who was thin, and I was neither.
The soap in the clamshell, gritty with sand, stung

like other shameful things:
when I dug my chin into my sister's unfused skull,
because my mother said be careful of her soft spot,

or when I licked the dog's face when I thought no one was
watching, to give him something he would understand.
The fur stuck to my tongue.

We were learning the one who has the power is the one
who cares the least,
cigarettes will kill you, blond is beautiful.

At the Grand Canyon, our mother wouldn't go near our father.

He wouldn't but just in case.

One day I'll lose my mind over a boy who won't
want me, and my mother will try to put me in perspective,
like a camera.
Imagine if I died
how much worse you would feel, she'll say helpfully.

I'll get skinny, everyone will think it's great.
Until a psychiatrist dispenses the pills that make me fatter,
and happier, and probably save my life. I'll tell her

there was a time when one of us was always crying, except
for the youngest, who said
Sometimes I wish I could care, but I just don't.
So this was her power, finally arrived.

Before Every Moon Was a Supermoon

I thought it was like death, all the days
the same and no one new to kiss or ruin

your life. Parents sniping at each other
when the meat was undercooked,

red juice pooling into the salad greens,
or when bills were lost in piles at the kitchen table.

I used to get drunk just to make something happen—
have a good time, then suffer extravagantly the next day.

Twenty years old. Home for the weekend, straining
my neck on a football field with friends and a boy

I no longer loved, trying to witness a celestial event
that hadn't occurred since Shakespeare.

Something about the moon, but we missed it
for the clouds. My life was never more my own:

slept late, read poems, had a car and a library job
that paid $50 a week for books and booze.

I didn't think about my debts. On the field
we narrowed our eyes against the fog.

Can you imagine having to go to a job every single day?
we asked each other. We couldn't.

Fisherman's Quarters

Before it was a dive bar, men rented rooms for the weekend,
came in with creatures on ice—striped bass, fluke

or that pungent bluefish, awful even in butter.
All the men have pictures with fish in their arms, proud as fathers.

Don't tell them where you live, the owner advises my first night.
You don't want anyone walking you home.

Nights when there's a band but no crowd, I feel embarrassed
to clap, turn busy when the song ends, rustling the ice.

This was a whaling town, and we got them all. Melted the beasts
down for perfume and oil, wove the small bones into corsets.

You could use the whole animal, unlace your dress by what burned.
Perhaps not all. The ones who survived went deeper into the sea.

There are whales still alive in this world born before *Moby-Dick*
was written. Come upstairs and read it to me, a regular says

but not like he's counting on it. His third drink is free.
Fish: the same word for the subject and the violence done to it,

like *skin*. I set down a vodka warm and medicinal.
I have a generous pour. I am not always so careful—

like the child parading his catch down the beach; swinging
from his net: a blowfish, delicate and puffed as a dandelion.

He'd meant to practice mercy but had waited long. It stilled.
So he kissed the coarse and speckled back and then he let it go.

Against Nostalgia

There I was, my life
around me like a spilled drink,
at a party trying to have
a meaningful connection
with the family cat, and there, driven
down the canopied side streets
in someone's mother's minivan,
where I said *Dan is actually*
a really good drunk driver
and I meant it.

There was Sunday night full
of dread, drawing the dogwood
on our front lawn as the sun
set behind it, sketchbook due
in Art tomorrow. I used up
every sick day, all eighteen,
cooked Lipton soup, that yellow bouillon,
and dropped in an egg, the white
tendriling like a jellyfish in the broth.
All of my life still ahead of me—

I lived four blocks from school and didn't
always walk. The days were long

and uncruel: holiday assemblies
with the principal as Santa
and the one dreidel song, movies in June
when it was too hot to teach, *Rent*
in Health class to scare us about AIDS.

No one ever beat me up and no one
I loved deeply had died. Why then
the diffuse despair, narrowing
into my notebook one letter over another
over another so you couldn't read the well
of words *help help help fuck fuck fuck*.
I thought I wanted to be in love but really
I wanted something to do with my hands.

Practical Survival Tips for Women

A dog practices passive resistance during a tornado watch,
belly-down in the street. Unmoved by his owner's taut leash

or urgency. Still, my office closes early and I meet a friend
for the Nan Goldin show. For years I misremembered

The Ballad of Sexual Dependency as *Despondency*
but what's the difference? Those bruised thighs.

Someone kept using their camera's flash during the slideshow
even as we shouted in the dark *Come on!*

There's a lot to be sick of. Last night I searched
"practical survival tips for women" after watching a video

of a woman attacked in her home (Sunday morning, cartoons on).
Safety is an idea, but a fist is a fist. The search turns up a gift guide,

how to grind your own oatmeal, as if convenience is a lifesaver.
I take down the name of a self-defense class, but I'd look

ridiculous and anyway sprained my wrist forcing lavender
into the ground. With a spade, I scraped brick out of the loam.

I mean brown dirt that sprawls under homes in New Jersey.
I know my Swiss Army knife is good for nothing

but a corkscrew. Danger is often a gun
and I'll never have one. Last week a man

shot his wife one town over on the front lawn,
their kids watching. There are sunflowers piled

at the foot of the elementary school where she taught,
We Miss You and her married name. I once believed

I could keep myself whole by marrying well, but then,
strangers: the men we call crazy and the men we call cops.

When my phone fills with news of the latest disaster
my friend says throw it in the river. But I need it to talk to you.

This Is Just To Say

William Eric
Williams, son
of the poet-doctor, was my pediatrician
until I was four and he died.
He gave me
a chicken pox shot
and a sticker for being brave
while my mother told him she knew
the poem about the plums
by heart.
He said
that wasn't really a poem,
just a note for his mother. In the blue
house on Ridge Road I was knocking
my heels against history,
oblivious.

I was eating a cherry lollipop and affixing
the sticker to my velvet dress, ruining the feel.
His father hated and loved our town
as much as I would one day.

A very bad environment
for poets,

he called it, and that was when we were still
a bit pastoral. I never saw chickens,

none that were living,
                                        and the only wheelbarrow
was symbolic, red, chained to a tree outside the library.
We had plums in our yard
                                                    and crab apples,
until all the trees
                                    got brown rot. Not quite
three square miles, a dry town, a blue line
was painted between the yellow on the road
outside the police station.
                                                I went to school
with the children of too many cops.
Their houses didn't grow any flowers
the year after college when
                                                    I came back
and

            would get drunk across
the railroad tracks where bars were
permitted, go home with men
who'd once starred

in school plays.

Backstage

I'd silently hand over

the costume changes. Like me they lived

with parents but had finished

basements, etc.

On very clear nights

on the porch of the bar, waiting

to get drunk enough to kiss someone,

I could see

the moon rising over the stadium

in the distance. It was renamed for an insurance

company but who wouldn't rather

imagine giants.

Mike

I fall in love and don't write a good word for weeks,
astonished into happiness.

I stop eating meat because he doesn't

and read a novel with the Knicks game on,
though Mike says he's too high up in the stands to see.

I keep it on just in case.

The way he loves me:

wakes me with egg sandwiches
and says hey that poem

you wrote about your ex
is really good.

An Incomplete List of What I Can't Tell You

Why live oaks aren't called *oaks*,
and whether all moths splay their wings open at rest,

or if some hold theirs closed like crossed legs.
Whether *nonplussed* is surprise or its absence.

How to make a fire. Why we say *ripped* to describe a body
that's muscled and whole. Whether to believe those who claim

they've seen an eastern cougar upstate, though scientists know
they're extinct. Why it was a ghost cat before it even died.

What I said to my dead grandmother in the dream when she strode
through the door on Thanksgiving and asked for a plate.

I was worried she couldn't eat and would be embarrassed. How she said
You were wrong, heaven is real. What I'd feel if I could believe it.

What it meant to my grandfather to hunt deer after the war.
Statistical odds and if three people in my family have fallen

down cellar stairs to their deaths, whether it's more or less likely
to happen to me. What kind of fruit tree we stood beside when

my mother said the skin cancer on her arm was nothing to worry about.
She snapped off a cluster of twigs and held it out like a chicken foot.

All our fruit trees are dying. Whether it was crab apple or pear.
Why *ravenous* refers to neither ravens nor ravines. The moon's name.

I thought every moon in autumn was a harvest moon, but I lived in a city
and never grew my own food. What did I know of the harvest?

You Should Feel Bad

The yoga studio near Mike's apartment has chalked outside
NOURISH YOURSELF // FEED THE WORLD

It means nothing. Yoga is nice—a pull in the thigh, your hip letting go—
but what feeds the world includes soy, vegetables, and animals (sorry).

I walk faster when I refuse a homeless man a dollar. I feel bad
when I buy coffee in a plastic cup, so I feel bad nearly every day.

When my friend cheated on his wife, the other woman
said *I have nothing to be sorry for*.

Yes, it's more my friend's fault, but isn't there enough
sorry to go around?

My mother writes to a murderer, worried he lacks books.
He calls the prison his university, mails my mother villanelles to type.

Tenderness can be unbearable. When Mike dances
to our favorite local commercial to make me laugh,

I know we're living in the good years. All of our parents
are still alive, and so are we, and the family dog.

How much time do we have? I confess I love being
lazy. Supine with a book and something to eat.

The word *fat* used to hurt me so much. Even in a book, innocuous
enough: a fat woman waited for the train. It pained me.

Like crying in Old Navy, trying on swimsuits before the pool party.
I wouldn't wish sixth grade on anyone. I try to keep alive in my mind

Dylan K., a fourth grader in my mother's school, who
when punished by the lunch aides for something that wasn't his fault

said *You're assholes, and I'm leaving*. And he did, he walked right
out of school, an act I can only call sublime. Perfect as a ladybug

that doesn't get killed, spared for being festive as a party dress.
It isn't fair. I say my friend's stepmother is *actually a dumb bitch*.

She voted for Trump, still it's like something out of a man's mouth
and not anyone I'd sleep with. For that, I'm sorry. Sorry—

always on my tongue. Women apologize for the accidental touches—
pocketbook swinging widely, hand sliding down the subway pole.

A chorus of *sorrys*. I love it when we're careful
because the world is not careful with us.

What's braver than a girl walking alone at night?
The only stars that cut through are the brightest

and sometimes they're not even stars.
The future humans won't see this night sky,

certain constellations drifted into the cosmic soup.
When they read our maps will they believe us,

and will they be here, puzzling the charts, reading anything at all?
For now, everything is still possible. The tunnels honeycombing the city,

the reef of train cars sunk into the Hudson. Oysters haven't yet
but might someday return. I want to feel bad and I want to get better.

One Year Off Generic Zoloft

I thought this sickness was another
Thing I'd outgrown like asthma or god
I thought my brain was well and whole

Because I made it so
No longer twenty and cringing
Drunk and crying

When I went off the meds
I still rose and went to work each day
Call it fear of failure call it moon

In Virgo ashamed of every word
I'd ever said or wrote woke blushing
In the night heart in my throat

Then I get good news and feel
Naked I get more
Good news and vomit

Mike asks with pity
And impatience *What would happiness*
Look like for you?

I guess being left alone for a year
Accountable to no one
But my fig tree and library fines

It might look like money
I'm not sure it looks like marriage
But still find myself saying about friends

They must be more in love than we are
Look at them making decisions
And smiling at City Hall

The boring thing is I recall
What happiness looks like
Oblong blue bitter on the tongue

The answer to a question
I've forgotten and invented
In 1991 like me

Gentle or Not

After we leave New York, I read a book about how not to
let the internet destroy my brain. I think
the answer is to have been raised in California,

to be a completely different person. At home
people clap every night for healthcare workers.
They clap like someone who's seen their friend's play

or flown in a plane when planes were still new.
I call it sweet but don't know how to judge
public gestures, like when after the towers fell,

after our mother pulled us out of school,
my little sister chastened me:
You shouldn't be reading right now.

My friends take me canoeing in the Housatonic River,
where the drought is obvious, water low
and undressing the downed trees.

Steve noses his canoe through narrow channels
of branches. I break through brutely, scraping
the belly of the boat against water-softened

trunks while a beaver slaps toward us, as if injured.
Steve says she's luring us away from her babies,
den entrance exposed by the dropped waterline.

I'd like to be able to look at a thing and know
what I'm seeing, the way my friend points an oar
at a pile of rocks and sees the trestle it once was.

Spring is working on me. I don't want to
change yet, but fawns and goats and all the girls
I knew in high school tell me it's time to have a baby.

I might listen or else settle for a dog
so large we name it Bear. When it finally
rains, the house shakes with thunder, wine

glasses chatter coldly and moss on the trees
brightens like wet velvet. I think I'm all
right but in dreams my teeth shatter.

The gardeners tell us to weed to protect
the new flowers. Every time I hear that word
I remember teenage friends—boys blowing pot smoke

at a spider trapped in the middle of its web,
        until it seized up and died. When I imagine
                children, I want boys who are gentle or not at all.

I pull at crown vetch until there are ticks in the crooks
        of my arms. Mike says we'll have them whenever I want.
                But I want too many things. Babies, yes, but also

to eat pizza in the street with unclean hands, unworried.
        I want to know the world the way my mother does, sprouting
                nasturtium seeds on damp paper towels in the kitchen.

I tend my own but cheat, buy them full-grown from the nursery,
        leaves round as saucers, in the way of daughters fearing
                their mothers like them less each year we grow older.

Controlled Burn

Seven trees come down
and then the trees are burned
to rid the yard of branches, brambles.

Smoke drifts thick through the coat
of the German shepherd who belongs
to the tree cutters. He snaps a twig

that an hour ago hung in the sky.
He breaks it, joyfully mossing his mouth.
It makes the sound of biscotti.

This morning in the house where Mike grew up
I pointed at a trapdoor outside our bedroom,
leading to an attic we've never seen.

He said three times *I feel like I'm going*
to wake up. We sleepwalk through the day
to the dull whine of the chainsaw.

We know now trees are social creatures,
feeding sugar to the young
and the sick through their roots.

They can keep alive a cut stump for decades—
the time it will take the collagen
to abandon my face and cartilage in my knees

to grind down to nothingness.
When I was a child, afraid of dying,
my father told me there was no heaven

but we stay in the earth, alchemize
into trees. I can't tell you the horror
I felt then, having expected angels.

The smoke thins from a billow to a plume
while the men turn trunks into logs
and the dog works over a new stick.

He was named for a city in New York
that was named for an ancient city
that burned, but he doesn't know.

The dog loves his stick the way I love
my mind, worrying the same grooves
into whatever fresh thing he's given.

At the Lighthouse

Artists create for the future,
          but there's no longer a future,
the visiting artist lectures, his projected

          works patterning his face.
Sorry to break it to you.
          It was the winter of holding

oysters in my mouth,
          apprehensive; the weight
on my tongue like the glide

          of white jellyfish
we palmed as children,
          how we'd sometimes crush

them, extrude their broken
          bodies through the netting
of our fingers, or else admire

          translucent threads knitting
the cutlet together and let them
          go. Because they lacked legible

faces, attics to house a brain,
we couldn't pity them.
My grief then for this dead,

entangled whale
might be for its size, the rude
scale of the world.

The humpback was a year
when it was starved,
muzzled by fishing line,

and washed up at the base
of the lighthouse, as if it could try
its luck again on land.

Bristle-mouthed, blue-eyed, baby.
Shat upon by birds. Dorsal fin
wilted as picked wildflowers.

The worst part is cracked
skin, black gloss giving way
to something like drywall.

No, worse: the luster of aliveness
        gone from the still-open
eyes. No: ripped flank spilling

        the great skein of blue
intestine no one should have
        ever seen. Impossible to take

in the emaciated hulk all at once,
        or its story: if it died before
landing, or how long its mother stayed,

        whether she sunk to the floor
like a stoved-in ship, or lived and followed
        her calf until the tide pulled out.

Two of my friends give birth this week,
        long-waited-for babies
named years ago. I send books

        that foresee a future
(*when you grow up...*) and a hat
        shaped like a strawberry.

We like to think we're unique
in our capacity to love,
but animals with intricate, whorled

brains do cherish and mourn.
Sperm whales mother hard,
cluster in a shape called *marguerite*

to protect the young, nosing them
into the seedy center,
a crush of kin, whose flukes petal

outward toward orcas or my
own kind. Whalers would have looked
at this landfall with hunger.

Though a starved whale hardly serves
industry; oil always the point:
the point of harpoon and invasion

and black, slick birds and melting ice,
all for a substance wetter than water,
that makes the gears of the world turn.

If I am hungry, it is only
        to look. During the fall
migration I watched whales' shining

        backs emerge like my own
knees in the bath, their rolling flukes,
        callosities, and piebalding skin,

like the sycamores of my suburb.
        I wanted to see an eye breach
in recognition above the surface.

        Now I get my fill
of the eye, served raw, chapped,
        helplessly open before gulls.

It thrilled, the walk to the deathbed,
        and then it appalled. Necropsy
left a window cut into its flank

        where, a week after dying,
the calf was still letting
        its mammalian blood, red

as anyone's I know. Red
    as my cousin's, her recent
seizure, the bad Latinate one,

    how she bit her tongue
and the blood flooded
    her mouth, husband

shouting to the dispatcher
    Help me, my wife is dying.
Another person I love

    sends me suicidal
poems, swears it calms intrusive
    thoughts, that he won't act,

then emails a new poem
    that goes *I lied*.
But they both survive.

    I send each my least
gruesome whale photo,
    because I don't mean

to convey that the world
        is a shipwreck, only
that *I'm thinking of you.*

        Small offering from this
sandy scrap of land, my temporary
        home at the artist residency,

where we dig up clams
        and decorate with sea detritus,
horseshoe crab carapace adorning

        the coffee table. Drunken potlucks.
We play a game of questions meant
        to make us fall in love. I'm asked

What are you overthinking right now?
        and answer *The choice to have children.*
A painter says *I'll tell you the truth. You shouldn't.*

        She possesses the authority
of one who reels in squid at night;
        serves us the muscle cold, chopped in salad,

and paints shadows with the ink sac.
          Weeks later we return to
the watery bier where the whale's open

          mouth streams rot. Death
particulate enters our noses
          and touches us inside,

while fin bones push through skin,
          growing toward light.
A poet asks if we resent

          how humans keep going
into space when there is so much
          we don't understand

about female anatomy or what lives
          in the deepest trench. We do.
But there are whales in space.

          NASA greases rockets
with their oil and the gold
          record of the *Voyager* is drifting

in that other sea, inlaid
with the humpback's song.
A month dead, the whale is peeled

like a clementine, blubber
white as pith, matter that would
have been sliced thin, *bible leaves*,

and melted. Sclera of eyes eaten.
That night we throw a birthday party
and death enters our throats.

The sculptor returns
from the city, its galleries filled
with hot breath and congratulations.

The virus in his lungs
takes flight and closes
the distance between us.

We wheeze, fill up like dolls
forgotten on the shore, inner cavities
sopping up the tides. We leave

soup at each other's doors,
        poured into old yogurt quarts.
Shimmering chicken fat and floating dill.

        Suck at asthma inhalers, bitter
clouds dispensed from plastic
        spouts the color of bath toys.

Whales once formed the observable world,
        present as plastic. Not just candle, lantern,
holy oil, but piano key, dog food, sole of shoe.

        Whales constructed the idealized female form,
baleen of the mouth bound into corsets.
        Livers juiced for Vitamin A. A psychiatrist

asks after my liver, reminds me men
        are allowed two drinks per day, women
only one. But I want what the men get, always have.

        In class with the venerable
old poet and his favorites, I prattled on
        as much as those boys

who dismissed certain poems
as precious. I don't know why
I think of this, what is meant by precious,

when my lungs are growing knotted
wrack and razor clam. The doctor
never takes a family history,

so I don't invoke my grandfather's liver,
the sea change of liquor and cancer:
men can't get away with it either.

There's no medicine
as we wait for the virus
to pass through us like weather.

The new kind. Not the weather
we were born to,
but the weather we've made.

Categories of Guilt

It should be remembered that what follows are the stories of the survivors: one can only speculate as to what accounts of atrocity the thousands of dead took with them to their unmarked graves.

—Nick Caistor, foreword to *Nunca Más: A Report by Argentina's National Commission on Disappeared People*

As is well known, the return of the beloved
does not correct
the loss of the beloved

—Louise Glück, "Persephone the Wanderer"

Criminal Guilt:

If guilt can be given a name and set down fixed like a butterfly
to a board criminal is the simplest to assign
the first junta Videla the generals the second junta
the torturers who called what they did "work" the men
who piloted the death flights the Navy doctors who gave
the second numbing shot of pentothal to the people
unconscious and captive on the floor of the plane the same
doctors who then stepped into the back of the cabin
so as not to violate they said their Hippocratic Oaths
the soldiers who removed the clothes who pitched
the people unconscious and captive into the sea
General Massera: "I am responsible but not guilty"

Political Guilt:

The first post -dictatorship president who passed laws
Due Obedience and Punto Final protecting the torturers
following orders his successor who said:
"The past has nothing
more to teach us"
the ones farther from the center who never
-theless gave us the world we swim through the United
States Department of Defense Kissinger
the School of the Americas their methods their manuals
that caution "The universities play
a prominent role in the recruitment of terrorists"

Moral Guilt:

The messiest the most capacious category it holds all kinds
of inaction those who didn't intervene
as most of us would not have intervened
those who stayed who witnessed who watched
a woman dragged off the bus by her hair
Borges who welcomed
the gentlemen's coup
the wives of the torturers who after a long day's work
kissed their brows and cooked their meat and cleaned
the sweat and stink
from their underclothes
the wives proximal to power who feigned
boredom at their husbands' trials
faithful to the end they don't want to hear
about the instruments of electrical torture their husbands
wielded against soft skin
"Picana
picana
picana" one performs a yawn

Metaphysical Guilt:

Those who left by ship by plane
who pressed beyond the Southern Cone and all the stars
looked wrong
those who entered a detention center
and survived
my grandfather in the interview the year before
his death where he confessed
that when the military came for his children
they had been looking for a man with a typewriter
a man who had already fled

the shoppers in the mall
with the clandestine detention center lodged in its basement
where beneath cashmere and concrete the captives
carved their names
if the guilt of survival applies
to the living why not objects too
why not the planes
the air that did not hold
the rooms that were washed clean the wires and cables
that conducted the shocks
the picana charged on car batteries in the black field
of night the kidnappers' cars

Ford Falcons without license
plates auctioned off after the dictatorship
to anyone who wanted   a souvenir   linden trees
the bullet   the fire   the dogs   and their trained hunger
metaphysical means god   is called into the room
it does not mean   he answers

Generational Guilt:

For those of us who dwell   in the after
is guilt the engine   in the choice   to look   or not look
too closely   at the forces that let   us be born
what is felt by   the children   grown now
adopted into military families
who decline genetic testing
who both know   and don't   their origins
in the operating theaters   of death

the American poet   going blank   at the reception
when asked "What are your poems about"
"She's been writing about the Dirty War lately"
my friend supplies
the shame I feel
to have made history   into a project
it's not a war you know

wars are fought by armies   not union organizers   professors
farmers   college kids
it matters what we name it   it matters the words
like the teenagers who co-opt   the slang
of the torturers   the torturers who are so many of them
finally dead

"You don't exist"

the children who are still children

taunt each other innocently they will make

meaning of whatever

floats

in the ether

the ones

who would never

return

Calle Sin Cielo

Street Without Sky. Skyless Street. Street Without Heaven.

I hesitate over the translation, turning the foxed pages of my aunt's poetry.

The book abounds with absence. City without duende. Dogs without sleep. Daughters without mothers. Faceless people. Wells without ghosts.

What is there: dead birds at the foot of every door. Nightmares. Street dogs. Wind, always the wind, carrying ash. Metafictional references to the act of invention. The dead. The longed-for dead. The caravan of the dead.

*

I found it online from a seller in Madrid, the postage five times the cost of the object. The book takes three weeks to cross the ocean and be delivered to the tip of Cape Cod. It would be equally true to say it takes thirty-eight years to reach me, from the moment she held this particular copy in her hands, touched pen to pages once fresh and unspotted.

The book offers a mysterious inscription ending with *Bienvenido, amigo*, and a quick sketch of a man holding a guitar. My father's best guess is that this copy was given to an ex with whom she parted on good terms. That she marked a new chapter for them by calling him *friend*. Unnerving that for thirty American dollars, I stand inside their intimacy.

When I feed her words into the translation machine, Alicia becomes Alice. The pronouns default to male. The book begins *I was hand in hand with an idiot down that street with no name*. And I am the idiot trailing her, words foreign to me that should not be foreign. In my father's language, I only know how to live in the present tense and the simple past.

*

I am thirty-one this year, the same age she was when she published her book in exile—more than halfway through her life. I am trying reinvention. Stop drinking. Without a job, my days unhinge slowly, without dread. In this coastal town in winter, I mean to finish a book and finally look hard at the past.

When Alicia wrote these poems, she was only a few years out from the dictatorship. In surreal little boxes, sharp and brief on the page, she's an actor reciting a soliloquy while screams are heard offstage.

She doesn't say what happened explicitly, and I fear it's wrong to animate the dead—the poem an act of ventriloquism. I don't want to be lyrical about the suffering of others. Alicia was lyrical about her own suffering, though opaque. I want to say it plainly.

We ride the entrails of a story, she once wrote.

*

The night the soldiers seized them, Alicia was twenty-five, her brother Enrique sixteen. The soldiers had come looking for a leftist playwright, the children's father. The playwright had already fled to Spain, along with his wife and two of his sons. The soldiers took whoever was home.

*

I copy each stanza from the fragile, browning pages. I haul up her obituary and recast it in English. Then my grandfather's plays and the interview conducted the year before his death.

For brief moments, it seems that all the questions I've ever had about my family are answered in the depths of the search results. I fish them out and cut them open. Spanish feels within reach, until I hear it in a restaurant spoken aloud, alive, a volley I can't return.

Long ago in New York, before dishwashing shifts, my father taught himself English by reading the newspaper alongside a dictionary. And for fun, he adds, *Howl*. Learning the land he had come to. He was nineteen, neural pathways still plastic. His father never learned the new tongue, except for a few words here and there.

It's late. I should have started long ago.

*

Because my father is not afraid to look at the worst things men have done, I finally ask him *how*. What happened to her in the private rooms of the detention center? On the shuttered main street, deep in the off-season, my ungloved hand goes numb holding the phone. He sighs, then says she was tortured with electricity, but that she never discussed the ordeal.

At least not with her brothers, her father. I understand the humiliation of having a body, not wanting to name the parts that were violated and how.

In Guantánamo Bay, where my father twice visited as a journalist, the gift shop sold T-shirts branding itself "the Least Worst Place."

In Sing Sing, he once sat in the electric chair that killed Julius and Ethel Rosenberg. He was visiting the prison to report on New York reinstituting the death penalty. He regretted it, sitting in that chair.

*

This loneliness
drifting, pushed by the dirty air,

among tin monsters with three electric eyes.

*

Their brother Enrique wouldn't have called himself a writer, but he did have a project. For years he kept a scrapbook of newspaper clippings he titled *El Mundo Fue y Será una Porquería*. The World Is and Will Always Be a... Shitshow, is my best attempt. Disaster might work. The kind of stories he cut and pasted affirmed his sense of nihilism, the absurdity undergirding the world. Think: a poor man wins the lottery, finally can afford to see a doctor, finds out he's dying.

Think: a child enters a death camp and survives. He moves abroad and doesn't return home until his deportation twenty-six years later. This is when he discovers his name etched into a memorial to the disappeared. Daily he walks past a monument informing him that he did not in fact survive the camp. He died in 1977.

*

The first thing my father is always asked is where he's from. He gets asked in New York, New Jersey, the places he's lived longest, where he's grown old. In Argentina, cab drivers ask him the same. For as long as I've known him, my father has said *I have no country*, pledging allegiance to nowhere.

Last Christmas, I gave him a book by Bolaño, who claimed his children as his only home. And *certain moments, certain streets, certain faces or scenes or books that are inside me and that some day I will forget—that is the best one can do for a motherland.*

Alicia wrote *Mi patria es sólo un puerto.* My homeland is only a port. A place of departure. Yet also homecoming. She did one day return to Buenos Aires, to the same apartment from which she was kidnapped. Her father's office became her child's bedroom.

*

I have a country, though no faith in it. It might be fairer to say it has me because I can't imagine my way out of it.

I must have once had faith. How else could I have yearly made the Fourth of July cake, layered with whipped cream, cut fruit crudely representing the flag. Wilting through the long dinner, the strawberries bled into the white.

Then the thrill of fireworks wrenching open the night. Until I was eleven, I had a friend whose father set them off—Catherine Wheels, Screaming Meemies—on the beachfront of their house. Fireworks were illegal there, but he was a cop and had confiscated the contraband from others.

My grandfather used to tell his children it was better to be a thief than a cop. He never said it to me; I was young when he died, and we didn't share enough language to express thoughts in the conditional. My father made sure to say it to me, in English.

*

It's a Sunday afternoon and I've called him to ruin his day, dredging up the past. Through chapped lips, I ask for the end of the story. In front of me, men hunch in the bay in high waders, raking for clams.

My father sits in a den where I imagine he has the television muted to the news. He considers turning on the light as the room goes gray around him. *Today exile is a mild winter season.*

If nobody survived the detention centers, how did they get out?

He tells me *The junta wanted to operate in secret. And Abuelo was calling up foreign newspapers, saying what they'd done. His contact at the Vatican said, if we ask Videla to let your children go, he might kill them for spite. But it might work.*

One night, they were once again hooded and thrown into a car, along with two other captives. Felt the tires turning over dirt roads. When they were let out, they were told to stand still or be shot. They stood until they heard the tires spin, and then they stood some more. The darkness beneath their hoods must have had a different quality than the darkness in the air around them.

What cave in the universe have I gotten myself into tonight? Alicia once wrote.

*

Because they are brother and sister lost in a forbidding landscape, I picture them as Hansel and Gretel, escaped from the witch's house into a dark wood. The witch's motivations are easy to comprehend; she just wanted flesh. What the military apparatus desired was something else. They wanted to kidnap the mind of the country. And, also, they wanted flesh.

Brother and sister and two others walk through the industrial outskirts of town, past an elastic factory, to a small house in the distance, following a pinprick of light. When a man answers the door, he tells them the time—two thirty—and gives two cigarettes to share among the four of them. It must be a comfort then to have something to occupy their mouths, to carry their own small fires.

I imagine what they looked like after five days of being beaten continuously, and I imagine the man's face when he opened the door, but

I'm not going to describe it. I trust your imagination. The man said they were not the first to arrive on his doorstep in this way.

They walked until reaching a gas station with a telephone. The night watchman took one look and asked what had happened. *We were inside*, they said. He knew exactly what they meant.

*

When my aunt wrote these poems, Argentina was a graveyard she wouldn't enter.

Skeletons scattered over the land,
stone wedges,
memories of what we haven't seen,
exercises of faith and memory.

*

When she visited the states, I was a child. I didn't know she was a writer then, though all I did was read. We rode the ferry past the Statue of Liberty, to visit glancingly. She, her son, and my parents conversed all day in a language that was familiar but unmeaning as birdsong. It was strange to see my father have a sister, to think one could have a sister, the daily fact of it, and then be set adrift into the world, time zones and entire lives apart.

*

I want her voice in these pages because I love her poems, their yearning and strangeness, the insistent passage of birds.

Earlier, I quoted her line *What cave in the universe have I gotten myself into tonight?* to heighten the dramatic tension. I am uneasy with this impulse and the implication that she did anything to cause her own kidnapping ("have *I* gotten *myself* into"). Because she was at home in abstraction, it's sometimes hard to parse a scene, or to imagine why the speaker has begun. Here then is the untitled poem in its entirety.

The sea is too far
The night is only darkness
I know the air for these few lines
and certain people are just an improbable memory
I have forgotten the smell of newborn mornings
The constant challenge of your eyes is the only harbinger of a slight chill
and the moist earth, an image I have just invented

What cave in the universe have I gotten myself into tonight?

*

I'm reminded of Hansel and Gretel because of my American girlhood, my mother's voice: *Next to a great forest there lived a poor woodcutter with his wife and his two children...* I don't know if the story would have resonated with my aunt. I don't know the Argentine folk tales. But I do know that the country prides itself on being nearly "European," the "Paris of South America." In part referring to their architecture and opera, in truth it's a brag about whiteness. It is a whiter country than much of Latin America, due to a nineteenth-century genocidal enthusiasm.

And then, as many as five thousand Nazis were welcomed after the war, some secreted in by the Vatican. They retreated to the mountainous terrain of Bariloche in the foothills of the Andes, where glacial lakes reminded them of home.

*

A thought experiment my father likes to engage, as if tonguing the space of a tooth that will not grow back: the direction his life might have taken if not for his siblings' kidnapping. No exile, no New York. A wife and a life in Buenos Aires. When I went back with him, we were eighteen and forty-four, and spent long, wine-drenched asados with his childhood friends. I grew so bored of my own incomprehension that I brought books to those dinners. It hurt that he had little in common with them anymore, he said later. I was used to reading his face, but I missed this, didn't see a shadow when I put my novel down, and he stood over the parilla, flames licking the coals, singeing the chicken, its raw flesh more yellow than white. *You can't get chicken like this in the U.S.*, he told me, *this is real chicken*. Food, the most reliable source of comfort to us both.

*

And one spends the fingers and the mouth
in tasks imposed by fear,
the poor hands of human oblivion
and the mouth and the viscera,
the hours of life on the way to death.

This is how things happen,
sorry,
clumsily.

*

I read that *parilla* was one of the words tainted by the dictatorship; the torturers called the board that victims were strapped to the parilla. How many years it must take to hear the word and think only of its original purpose. Perhaps as long as it takes to restore a polluted river: a generation.

*

I remind him that to undo the kidnapping, more factors must change. All of the family would have had to flee at once. Or to stay, Abuelo would need to be a different kind of writer, ideally no writer at all. And still, if they had stayed and lived quietly, beyond the notice of the death squads, they would not be untouched by violence, only differently damaged. If not their own, they would have watched other people's children vanish and pretended not to see.

*

My father keeps his own book, a ghost he's been writing all my life that's never done. Sometimes I ask how the memoir is coming along, though he thinks *memoir* is pretentious, instead calls it *my text*, the least flashy phrase he can imagine. *I should send it to you*, he's told me for years.

Alicia appears in his text because he cannot write his life without her in it. Even though they didn't always speak. Even though she prized her privacy. *Would she hate that I'm writing about her?* I ask. My father says *No*, emphatically, but he is too long accustomed to giving me what I want.

*

In a poem titled "Europa," she imagines a fearful future

when my flesh will be anyone's
and my voice will shout from the mouth of another.

Then,
my country
will also be far away.

*

From far away, I say sorry for bringing all of this up. Ask my father what he's making for dinner, listen to him recount preparations for pork loin. There will be mashed potatoes. Rosemary? No rosemary.

He wants to know I am home before hanging up, because the streets are dark for us both, and I've just reminded him what people are capable of. We exchange goodbyes and I love yous, while I kick off my boots, granular sand and snow wetting my socks in the entryway. Her book waits at the center of my desk. I hold the back cover before the mirror, consider whether we look alike, and decide not. Alicia's round face and the dark curls falling over her eyes.

Then I look harder.

She looks like my father and I look like my father, but in different parts of our faces. We meet somewhere in the middle.

◊

Ida

The water entered twice: rose
from the cellar and fell
through the roof. In the guts

of the house, past the drop
ceiling, hundred-year-old
horsehair insulation

wet and furring the walls,
as if coming alive in the squall.
A horse reborn

out of water—a myth
never written down.

*

In the basement, my father,
ankle-deep, argued with the sump pump,
chancing electrocution.

We were going to lose it all:
doll house, children's drawings,
books, though not the crumbling

volumes my grandfather troubled
to send by ship. Maybe the water
remembered having spared them before

on their long, freighted trip
from Argentina to Spain. Perched high
on wooden shelves, basement sloshing below,

they were beautiful, leatherbound, purposeless:
no one we knew needed Hawthorne
or Beckett in Spanish.

Yet nothing made me feel
closer to my grandfather
than the necessity of translation.

One day, I'll be duty-bound
to keep a row, though I have
no permanent address. A house

at this moment seems a burden, breached
walls already beginning to bloom into mildew.

*

We bailed with mugs, floodwater
brackish as yerba mate.
People were drowning downriver

but we didn't yet know,
as we shifted through dripping
newspapers, real ones, with my father's bylines,

and then my invention of a hometown
paper where I drafted disaster:
A terrible fire in New York, over 103 people dead

I had never seen a fire,
but I was willing to imagine.
Back when we played

Would You Rather:
burn or freeze? fire or water?
I was never afraid of water.

The same question posed
when deciding where to live:

which natural disaster can you stand?

When my parents chose hurricane,
they thought there'd be no tornados,
but they touch down now and again,

like migratory birds
charting a new course.

*

Before hurricanes were named,
they were rare enough to be tagged by year,
as if devastation was only annual, if that.

The Great Hurricane of '38 swallowed houses
up the New England coast, churning mouthfuls of debris,
lamppost in the maw, almost jaunty as a pencil in a child's mouth.

A family in Rhode Island
climbed to the third-floor servants' quarters,
and when the roof was torn off them like a scab,

they found themselves in the ocean;

fashioned a raft out of ceiling beams
and sailed through the wreckage unharmed.

But the servants couldn't swim.

*

I was wrong to say that water
has designs, has the power to spare,
but it's hard to imagine force without

intention: water welling gutters, valleys,
soil, mouths. There is no hollow it will
not fill. If it were true that the water

remembered a crate of yellowed books
floated between countries, the flood
would recognize the water in all of us:

my neighbors downriver, washed away in their cars.
If it were true, the water would recall
the sightless sea they were made in

and it would carry them still.

Egg Party

The spring my systems go wrong, I throw a party
where the theme is eggs. Chicken eggs deviled

and overburdened. Caviar held precariously
to potato chip by a slick of cream.

The idea is rebirth, claim whatever rituals
remain palatable. Spring of resisting

augury, not interpreting what it means
that one part of my body wants

to kill another part. In the dark
socket of jar, the black roe teem.

Some people are nauseated by clusters:
a shucked pomegranate disclosing its cells,

studded face of a sunflower enough to swoon.
That's not what makes me sick. I spoon,

I scratch the blood from boiled egg halves
with a fingernail. I am now buzzing

with terrible purpose: white blood cells
assemble in my throat like a swarm

of ants taking down larger prey;
I'll be obvious and picture a butterfly,

the thyroid always described as a winged gland.
Meanwhile, I go on chopping dill and tapping

eggs open against the sink. My friend, a twin, helps peel—
cracks a double-yolk and misses her sister.

This spring, in the forest, a small bird hooked onto my palm
with devastating trust. Two sunflower seeds slotted into her beak

as I fit into my life, almost comfortably,
almost equal to the task, the daily braveries required.

At the party where no one is heartbroken, there's a touching
fidelity to theme. The florals and golds. The small wants.

Egg whites fizzing the whiskey in our cups.
The possible fish popping against teeth.

Currency

after Ellen Bryant Voigt

we're going to marry next year try
for a baby and still what to do with my love's
unhappiness sure I give decent advice
but it doesn't help find a real therapist
I implore when he misses

mountains the effort sweat of ascent
misses the owls and the yearling bear
who pressed his face against our door
to better taste the air

does not love the sea does not
love his work he is aware
that everyone from his old life
makes more money than us
first home second home month in Italy

it pains him not the money but the idea
that we've failed it must hurt I know
but you can't respect money
so much I say it's wonderful
to have but it doesn't deserve *respect* neither

of us will ever out-earn our fathers so what
our kids will take loans if there's still
college then I took loans they can too
the thought does not cheer him I know people

with money they leave blood-stained
underwear on the floor for the maid
they tone their bodies all day long they fly
to Fiji and still their children starve themselves
they are desperately unhappy they looked
at me like I was a fertility statue
                                                    none of their mothers

had breasts remember we're doing okay
you gave me a diamond scientists grew
inside a lab I love it more than I thought I would
I have rocks for you too from the sea
they are ten thousand
years old these are our savings

Socrates with Fleas

After his mom dropped him off
he attacked his tail like it didn't
belong to him. So I scooped him up

ten pounds of resistance in my arms
and Mike applied the chemical potion
careful not to sting his eyes while

I held him in the tub like a baby
on my chest facing the world
flea shampoo running down our legs

while the dog named for a philosopher
tried to flail out of my arms like a caught fish
at the bottom of a boat his last chance

before being gutted. Watery
in certain lights he is more
like a furtive land-bound prey.

His rabbit heart leapt into my palm
slamming the wall of his grizzled chest.
He was wary of Mike for two days

but I was the favorite—followed
from couch to bed to toilet
as if I were protecting him

as if I hadn't been part of it.
I read the Galway Kinnell poem
where he says to his infant

I think you think I will never die.
Children grow up but dogs never have to.
Socrates thinks nothing

ever dies not even the gecko
he catches in his jaw—
once in all his years of chasing.

He learns you can swallow
the tail and the lizard still
escapes with his life.

A year later Mike thinks
he came up with the name
Socrafleas. No

I have to tell him
I invented it and you
were so impressed with me.

Poem for My Children Born During the Sixth Extinction

The first things kids learn in school are the seasons.
By now they already know their colors, maybe even their addresses.
My children will learn *hurricane* and *wildfire*. It is summer

and then it is winter. They won't know the sweet weeks
of early June, honeysuckle, wearing a sundress without sweat
pooling behind a knee. Maybe even a little cold at night.

They might not know bumblebees, not personally.
Polar bears they'll read about like dinosaurs.
We'll still have the old-fashioned disasters: broken elbow, split lip.

I'll try not to scare them, but when I see them eating unwashed grapes
I'll tell them about pesticides. One will forget but the other won't eat
fruit for years. When they ask if I believe in heaven I will lie.

When they're little I'll want them to feel safe.
When they're older I'll want them to believe their bones
will lie dumb in the earth forever. This is your one life.

They'll want to know what their parents did before they were born.
We had dinner parties. Traveled a little, not enough.
Read our friends' books. Had a dog they won't remember

but will pretend to, and too many plants. Water-damaged
the windowsill and lost our deposit. When our spider plant mothered
into twelve stalks, we potted them, called them the spiderettes.

They were supposed to be housewarming gifts, but we didn't
know twelve people moving. We tried not using too much
plastic, not eating too much meat. It didn't matter.

We knew our children's lives would get worse every year.
We thought they might like to be here anyway,
to know oceans, ice cream, optic nerves, the flowers and all their names.

Pokeweed

A small stalk, it grew in the alarming
way of tumors, grew as if dreamed.
It was hard to see the problem at first,

weeds sprung within my mother's rosebush,
like spotting the flaw in an emerald.
There's talk of selling the house,

which needs a new roof, and I take
my reluctance into the garden.
I am trying to reverse years of disregard,

trying to care for the plot that raised me,
where my lavender died as soon as it was bedded,
though the lamb's ear held on for some seasons.

Bound in ivy, beneath the evergreens, crouches the unsettling
statue of a boy, Buddhalike but not the Buddha,
skull preternaturally round, gifted by an ex.

I led him past the gate, knelt in the tall grass,
didn't feel the mosquitos until later.
Stray cats lapped rainwater on the pool cover.

Before it was drained, I swam naked
and sometimes fully clothed;
when you're a child, novelty is the point.

I don't know if I was happy but here is where I was.
On the back stoop, hunting meteors with my father:
I was ten, it was winter, we could see our breath.

Now I dig into the ruts between brick,
chasing the fleshy taproot down
to where the dirt changes color.

I uproot all but wild
strawberries, tiny and crystalline,
perfect for the dollhouse lost to a flood.

I know conversation with the land only goes
one way. But when I pull at the weeds,
the weeds, I think, pull back.

Notes

This Is Just To Say: William Carlos Williams spoke about his relationship to the town of Rutherford in an interview with *The Paris Review*, Issue 32, Summer-Fall 1964.

At the Lighthouse: The phrase "watery bier" is borrowed from John Milton's "Lycidas."

Categories of Guilt: The first four categories of guilt (criminal, political, moral, metaphysical) are taken from Karl Jaspers's *The Question of German Guilt* (Fordham University Press, 2001). Jaspers was a German existentialist philosopher who categorized and defined various forms of collective and individual guilt following the Holocaust. I use these designations as a container for considering the Argentine military dictatorship of 1976–1983; however, the last category is my own.

The first epigraph is from the English version of *Nunca Más: A Report by Argentina's National Commission on Disappeared People* (Faber and Faber Limited, 1986, in association with Index on Censorship).

The second epigraph is used with permission: Excerpt from "Persephone the Wanderer" from *POEMS 1962–2012* by Louise Glück. Copyright © 2012 by Louise Glück. Reprinted by permission of Farrar, Straus and Giroux. All Rights Reserved.

Lastly, the poem owes a debt to *A Lexicon of Terror: Argentina and the Legacies of Torture* by Marguerite Feitlowitz (Oxford University Press, 2nd edition, 2011), an excellent book which I relied on heavily.

Calle Sin Cielo: The poem borrows its title from a book of the same name by Alicia Creste, published by José Matesanz in 1984. (Later in her career as a singer-songwriter, she went by Alicia Crest.) Unless otherwise noted, all italicized language is hers, and the translations (and any errors) are my own.

The playwright, my grandfather, wrote under the name Alberto Adellach.

"El mundo fue y será una porquería" are lyrics from the tango song "Cambalache" by Enrique Santos Discépolo.

I encountered Bolaño's comment about motherlands in *Roberto Bolaño: The Last Interview and Other Conversations* (Melville House, 2009).

The "Hansel and Gretel" line is, of course, by Jacob and Wilhelm Grimm.

Socrates with Fleas: The Galway Kinnell poem referenced is "Little Sleep's-Head Sprouting Hair in the Moonlight" from *The Book of Nightmares* (Houghton Mifflin Company, 1971).

Acknowledgments

Grateful acknowledgment is made to the editors of journals and other venues in which some of these poems previously appeared: *The American Poetry Review*, *Bennington Review*, *Best New Poets 2023*, *Cero Magazine*, *The Cortland Review*, *The Kenyon Review*, *Poetry Daily*, *Poetry Northwest*, *No Tokens*, *The Slowdown*, and *The Yale Review*.

The following poems, in earlier versions, first appeared in *You Should Feel Bad*, winner of a 2019 Poetry Society of America Chapbook Fellowship: "Sisters," "Fisherman's Quarters," "Against Nostalgia," "Practical Survival Tips for Women," "Mike," "An Incomplete List of What I Can't Tell You," "You Should Feel Bad," and "Poem for My Children Born During the Sixth Extinction." Thank you to the Poetry Society of America, Brett Fletcher Lauer, and Stephanie Burt for bringing the earliest seed of *In the Good Years* to life.

Thank you to brilliant friends whose insights, encouragement, and wise edits helped move the book toward its final form—especially Emma Hine, Tracy Fuad, H.R. Webster, Asa Drake, Kate Doyle, Victoria Kornick, Tess Gunty, and Ocean Vuong. It is an immeasurable gift to be read carefully by you. Thank you also to Ocean for excavating the title from within the manuscript.

Thank you to the wildly generous teachers from whom I've learned at schools, residencies, and conferences, who provided crucial reading recommendations and helped shaped my understanding of poetry: Mark Wunderlich, Deborah Landau, Matthew Rohrer, Meghan O'Rourke, Sharon Olds, Paisley Rekdal, Ada Limón, Eduardo C. Corral, and Monica Youn. I am grateful and lucky to have crossed paths with you.

Thank you to the New York University Creative Writing Program, the Community of Writers, Monson Arts, the Kettle Pond Writers' Conference, the Tin House Summer Workshop, and the Sewanee Writers' Conference for providing homes for this work. To the St. Botolph Club Foundation, whose Emerging Artist Award afforded me the opportunity to travel to Buenos Aires. To the Fine Arts Work Center in Provincetown for seven months to reimagine this book, and for employing me afterward. Thank you to these organizations' staffs and board members for all that you do to support artists—particularly Sharon Polli and Naya Bricher.

A warm thank you to the writers who read drafts of these poems across many years and workshops: Taneum Bambrick, Rhoni Blankenhorn, linda harris dolan, Ryan Dzelzkalns, Tyler Gonlag, Shelby Handler, Sophie Herron, Emily Hockaday, Carolina Hotchandani, David Hutcheson, Alisha Kaplan, Nicole W. Lee, Jen Levitt, Sara Mae, Eduardo Martínez-Leyva, Paco Márquez, Brian McCabe, Holly Mitchell, James Fujinami Moore, Madeleine Mori, Megan Pinto, Sahar Romani, Sarah M. Sala, Victoria Sanz, Jimin Seo, Raena Shirali, Matthew Spettell, Avia Tadmor, Weiji Wang, and Alison Zheng.

To the wonderful team at Four Way—Martha Rhodes, Ryan Murphy, and especially Hannah Matheson—thank you for helping me realize a lifelong dream.

To Sean Landers for allowing his beautiful painting, *Sperm Whale Skeleton I* (2023), to grace the cover. I can't imagine a more fitting image for this book.

To S Emsaki, dear friend and advisor on all things visual art.

To Erica Drew for a conversation that inspired "We Love Bad Dogs."

Deep gratitude to my family for their love and willingness to appear, however refracted, in these pages. Thank you to Camilo Bayona for permission to quote from his mother's poems. To my father, Esteban Creste, for sharing his stories and checking my translations. To my sister, Allegra Creste, for being a smart and honest reader. To my mother, Marie Creste, for keeping my newborn held and happy as I finished final edits. To Michael Sarinsky for understanding me and this book so well and for words that made all the difference. And to Julian River, my whole heart.

About the Author

Laura Cresté is the author of *You Should Feel Bad*, winner of a 2019 Chapbook Fellowship from the Poetry Society of America. She holds an MFA from New York University and has received fellowships and other support from the Fine Arts Work Center in Provincetown, the Sewanee Writers' Conference, the Tin House Summer Workshop, the Community of Writers, Monson Arts, and the St. Botolph Club Foundation. Her work has appeared in *The American Poetry Review*, *Bennington Review*, *The Cortland Review*, *The Kenyon Review*, *Poetry Northwest*, *The Yale Review*, and elsewhere. She lives in western Massachusetts.

We are also grateful to those individuals who participated in our Build a Book Program. They are:

Anonymous (5), Robert Abrams, Debra Allbery, Maggie Anderson, Jean Ball, Sally Ball, Adria Bernardi, Richard Blanchard, Laurel Blossom, Lee Briccetti, Anne Babson Carter, Jennifer Christman, Aaron Coleman, Peter Coyote, Elinor Cramer, Michael Anna de Armas, Brian Komei Dempster, Patrick Donnelly, Lynn Emanuel, Joan Frank, Rigoberto Gonzalez, Elizabeth T. Gray Jr., David and Joan Grubin, Naomi Guttman and Jonathan Mead, Beth Harrison, Jeffrey Harrison, KT Herr, Carlie Hoffman, Elizabeth Jackson, Linda Susan Jackson, Marilyn Johnson, Deborah Jonas-Walsh, Maeve Kinkead, David Lee and Jamila Trindle, Rodney Terich Leonard, Jen Levitt, Howard Levy, Owen Lewis and Susan Ennis, Ralph and Mary Ann Lowen, Maja Lukic, Ricardo Alberto Maldonado, Cleopatra Mathis, Victoria McCoy, Lupe Mendez, Mary Jane Nealon, Nicole Nevadunsky, Kimberly Nunes, Cathy McArthur Palermo, Veronica Patterson, Eileen Pollack, Martha Rhodes, Soraya Shalforoosh, Sarah Stone, Yerra Sugarman, Marjorie and Lew Tesser, Reed Turchi, Maria Walsh, and Calvin Wei